GW00514667

true love is...

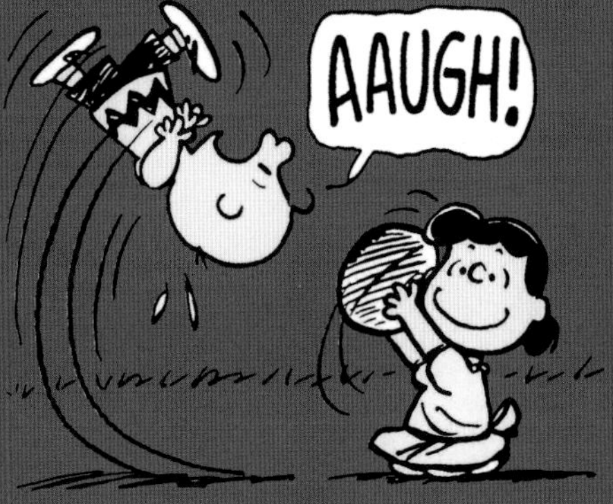
AAUGH!

complete trust

by Charles M. Schulz

This edition published by Ravette Publishing 2006.

ISBN 10: 1 84161 259 6
ISBN 13: 978-1-84161-259-1

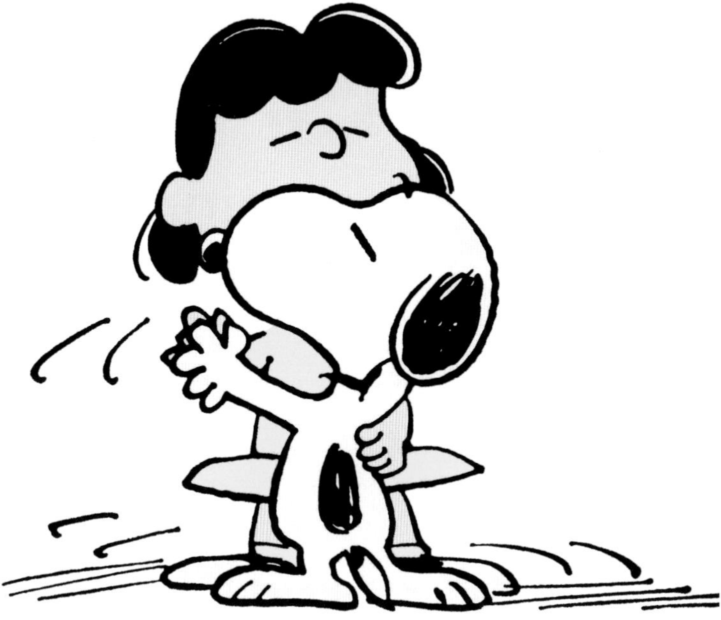

RAVETTE PUBLISHING

love is

doing things together

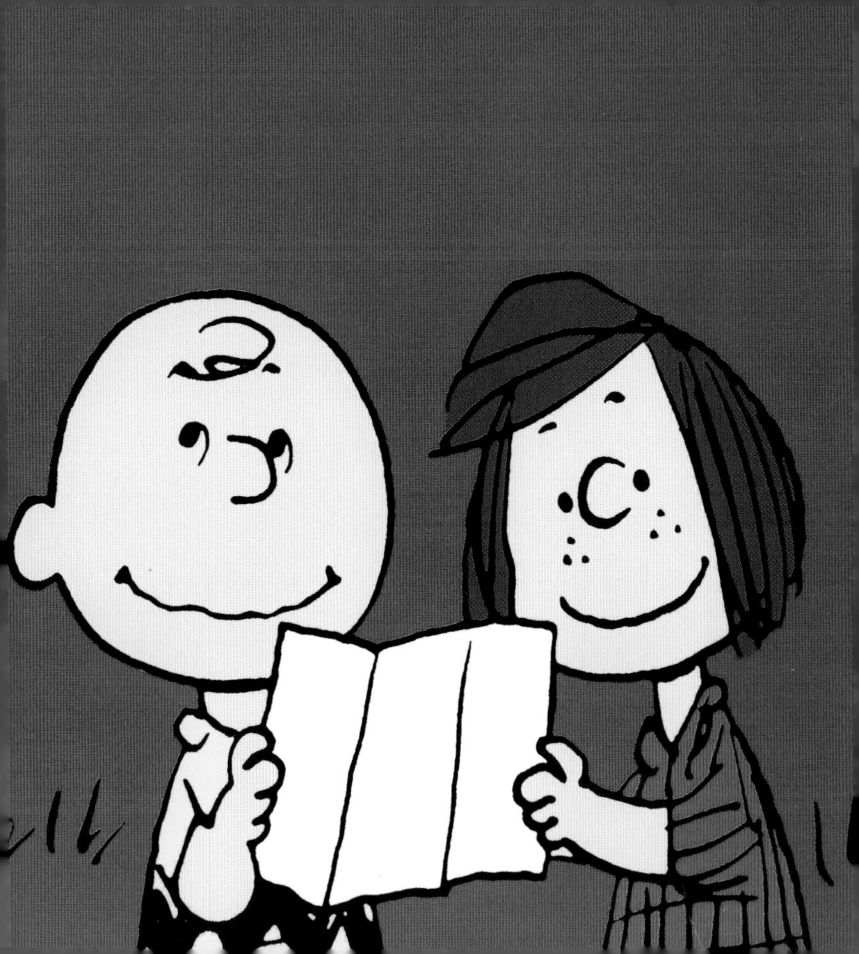

love is

wondering
what he's doing
right now this
very moment

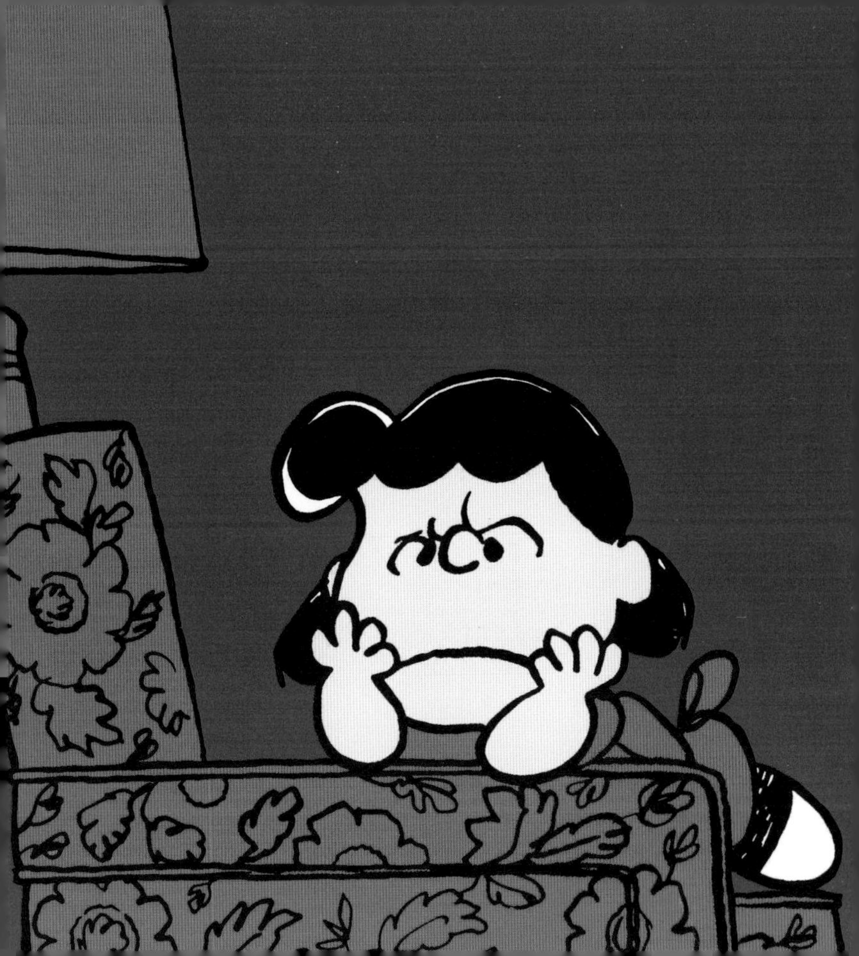

love is

being a
good loser

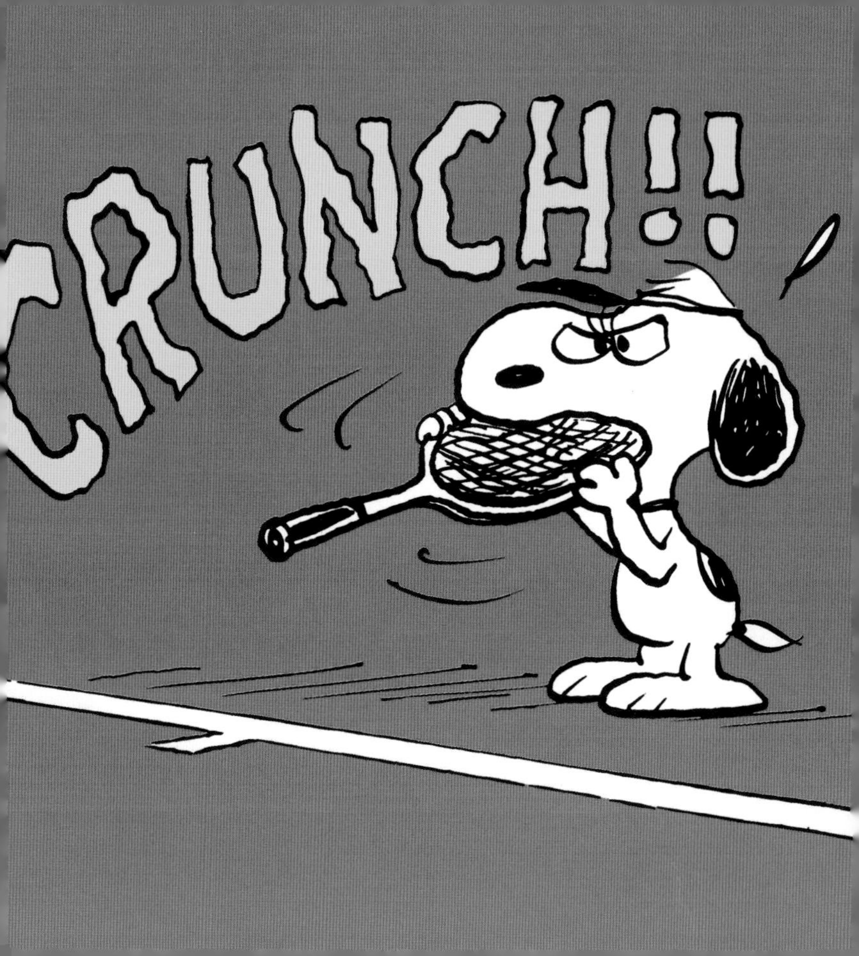
CRUNCH!!

love is

buying
somebody
a present with
your own
money

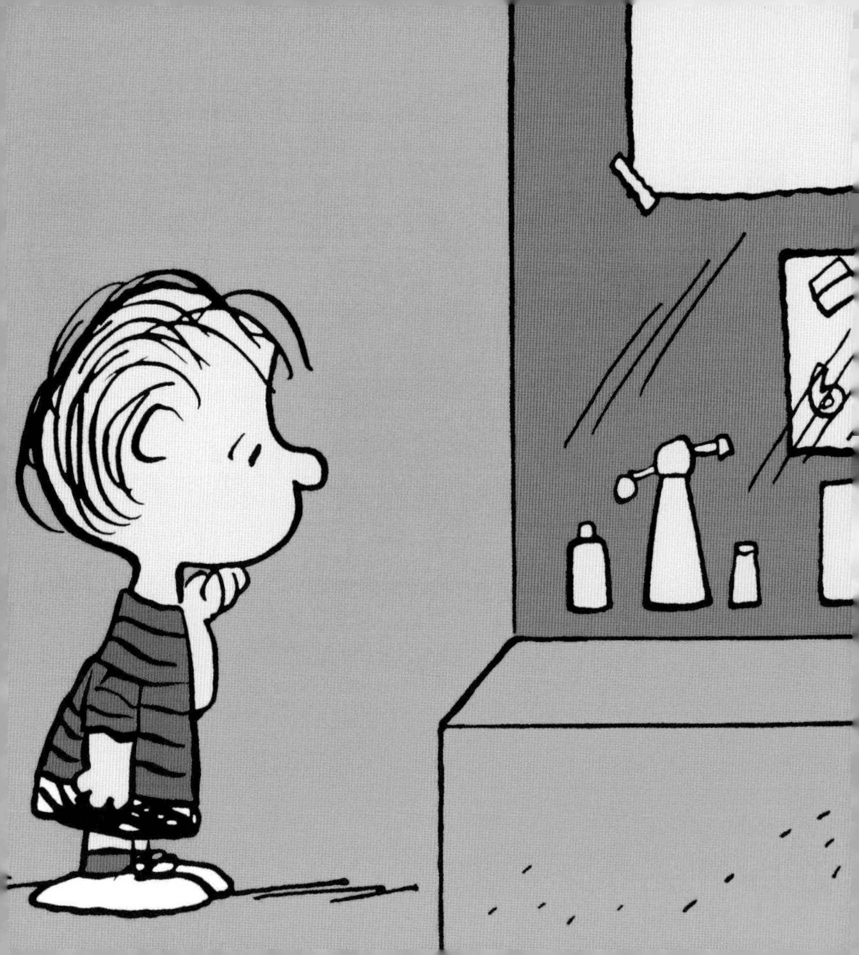

love is

being

hospitable

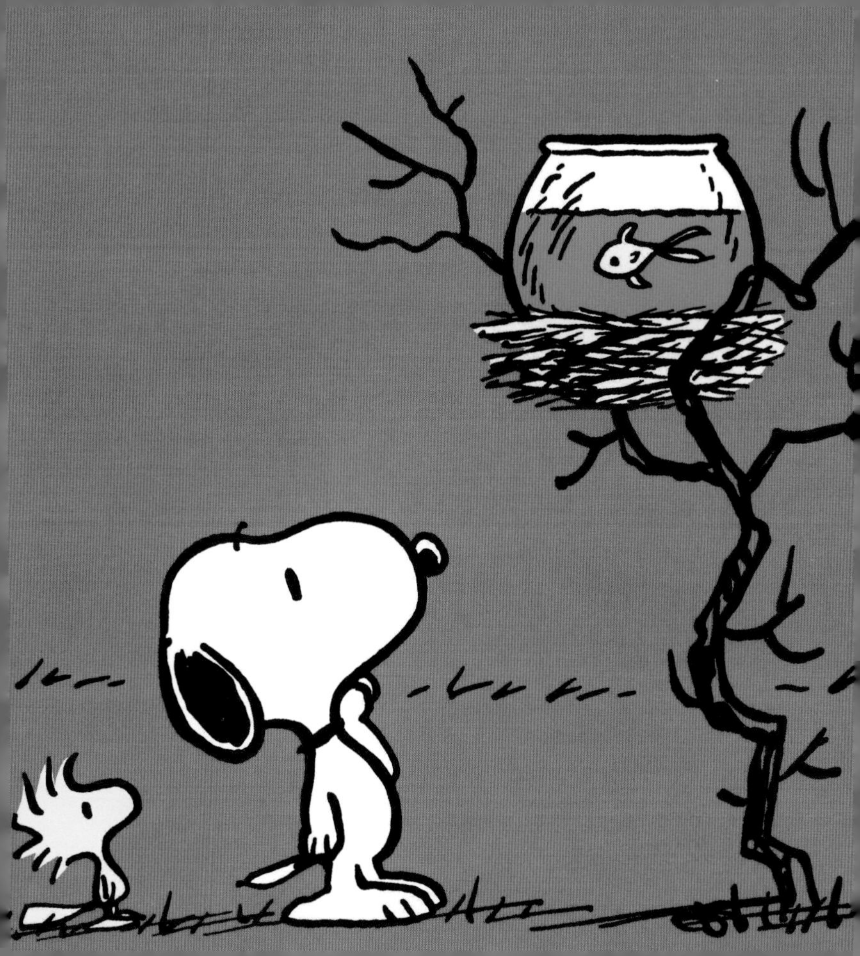

love is

letting him win
even though
you know you
could slaughter
him

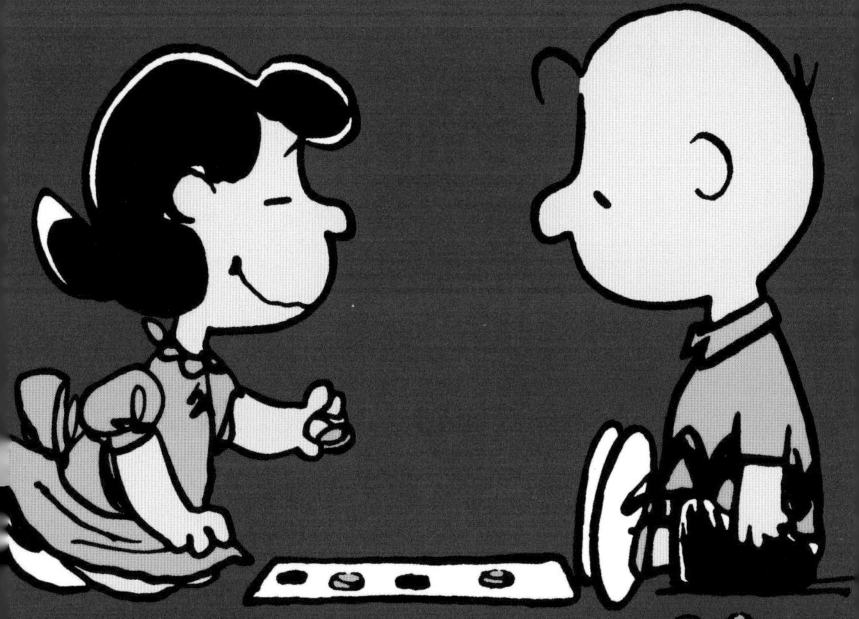

love is

being happy
just knowing
that she's happy
. . . but that
isn't so easy

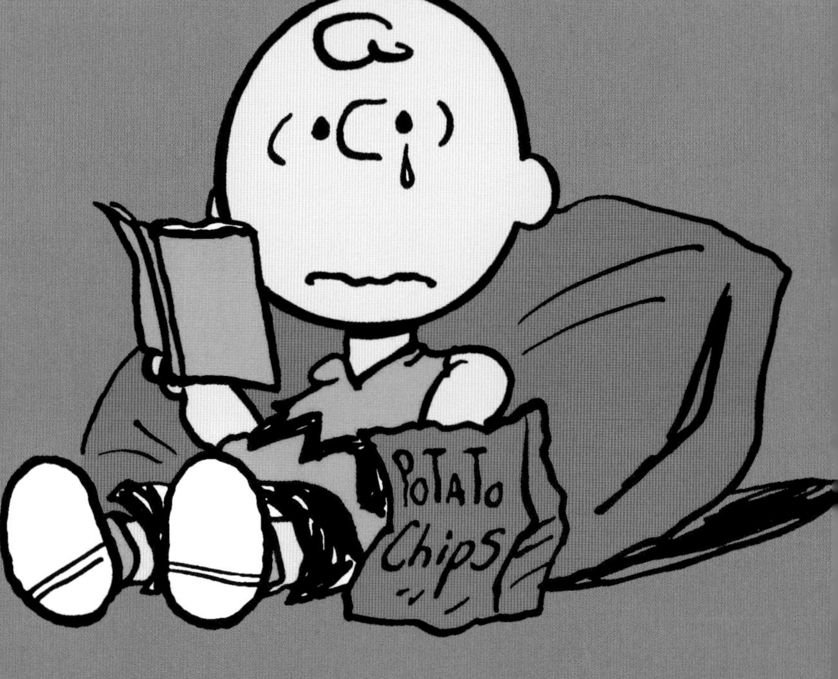
POTATO
Chips

love is

dressing up
for someone

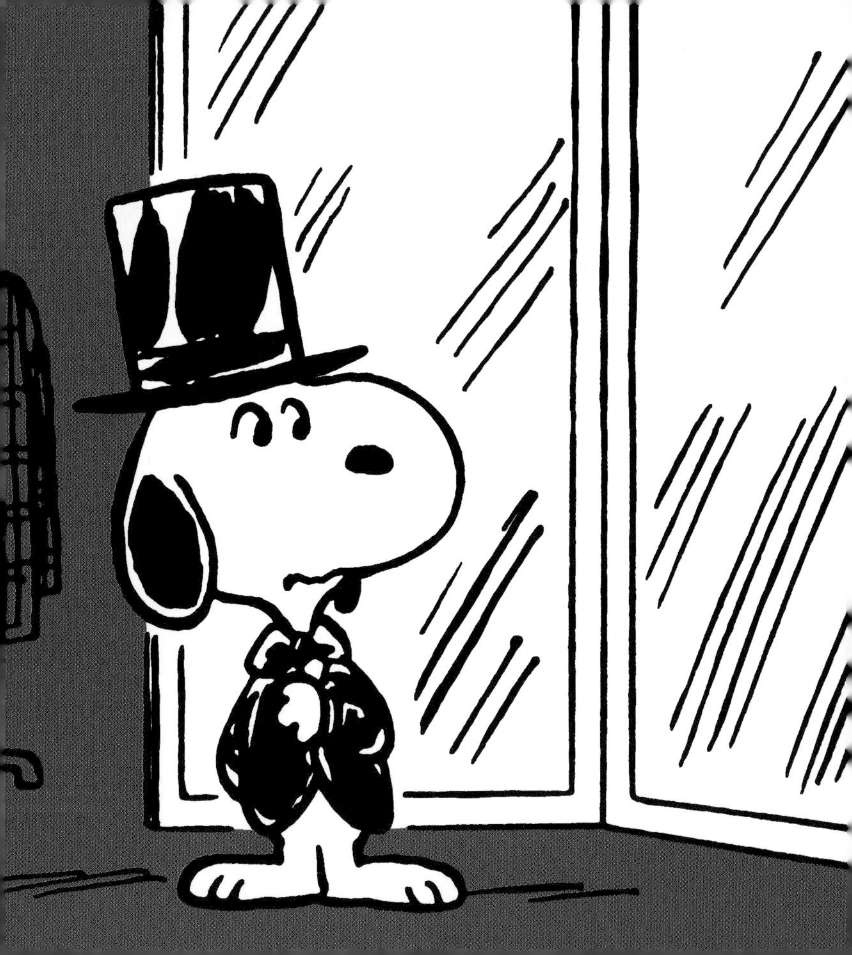

love is

a push in
the right
direction

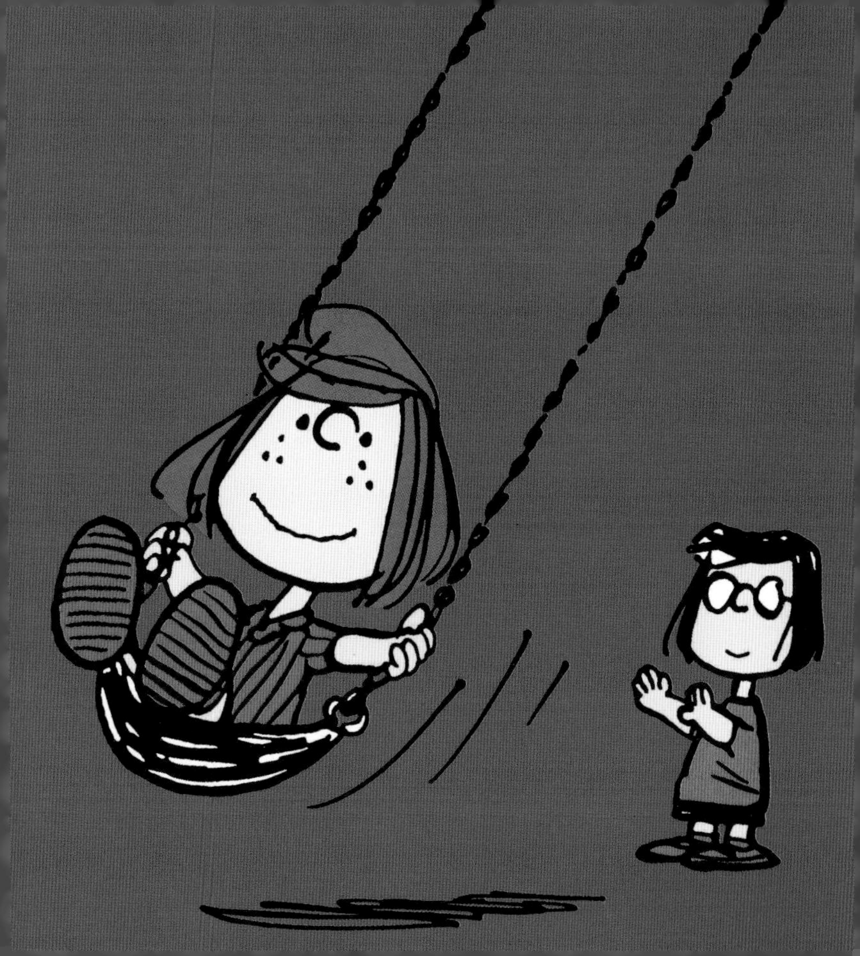

love is

not nagging

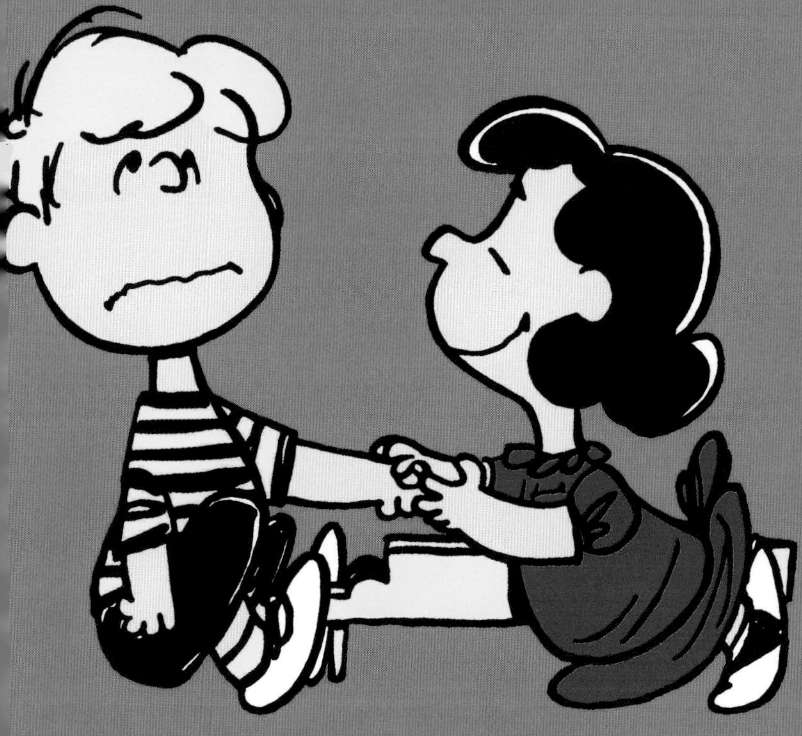

love is

being faithful
to the very
end

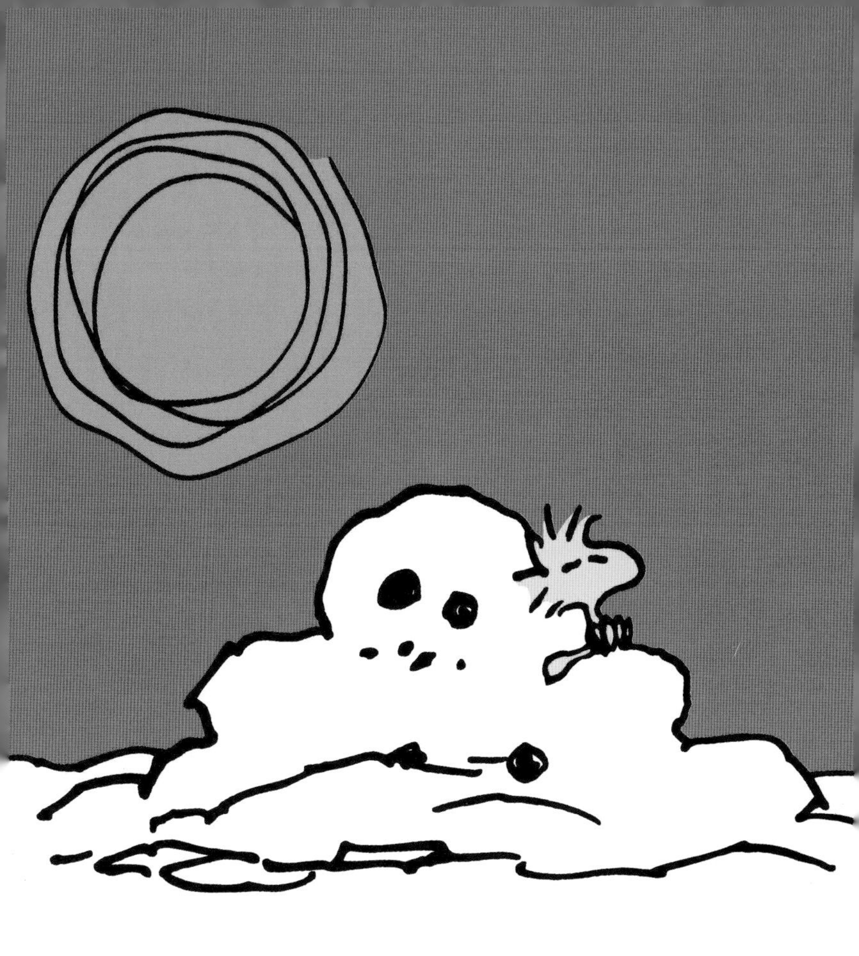

love is

when your
friends invite
you to be guest
of honour

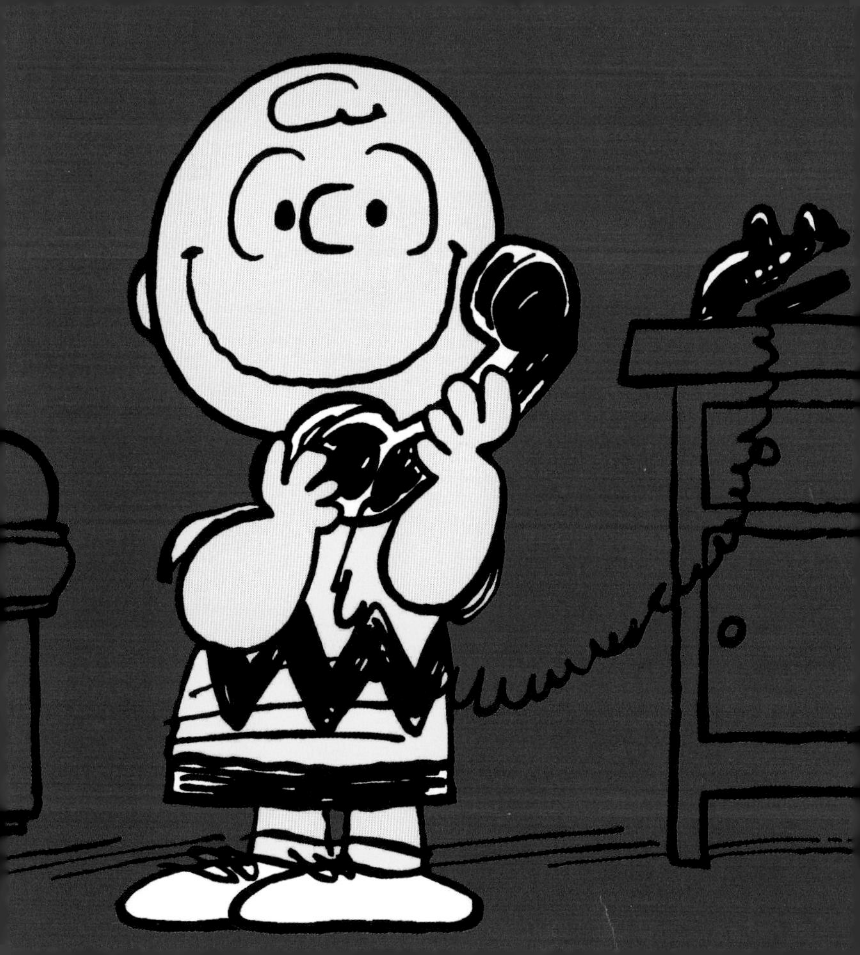

love is

tickling

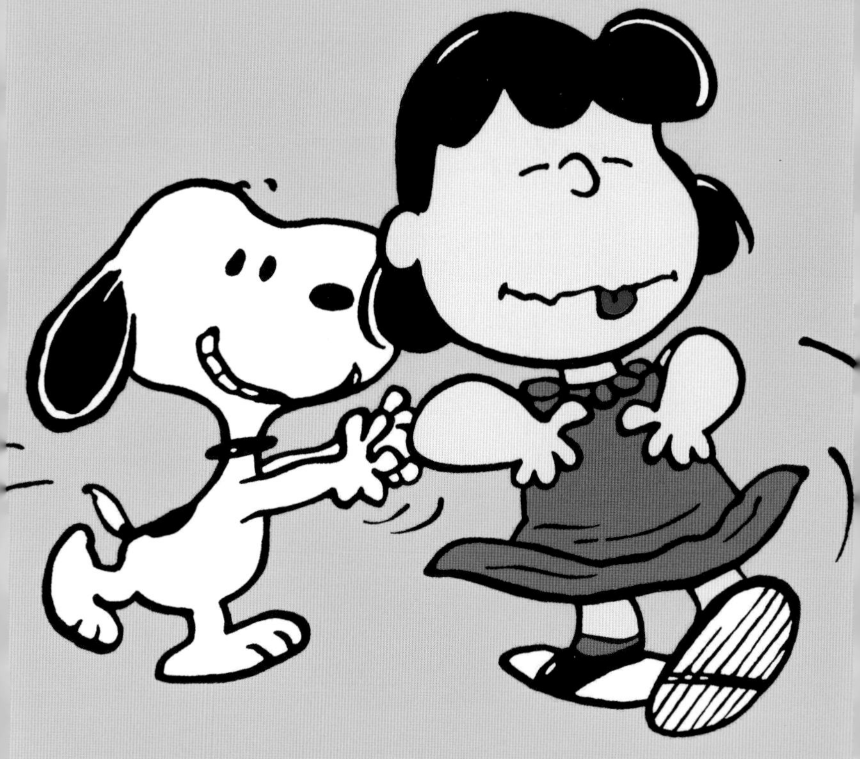

love is

an invitation
to lunch

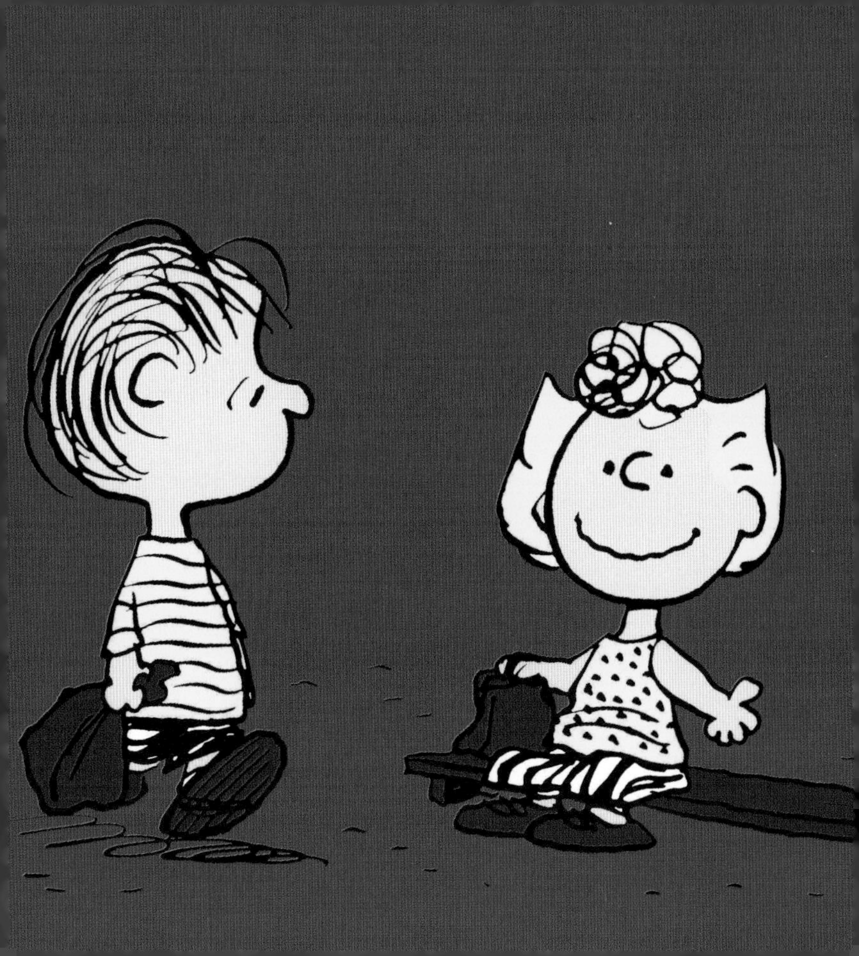

love is

allowing
someone to
sleep late

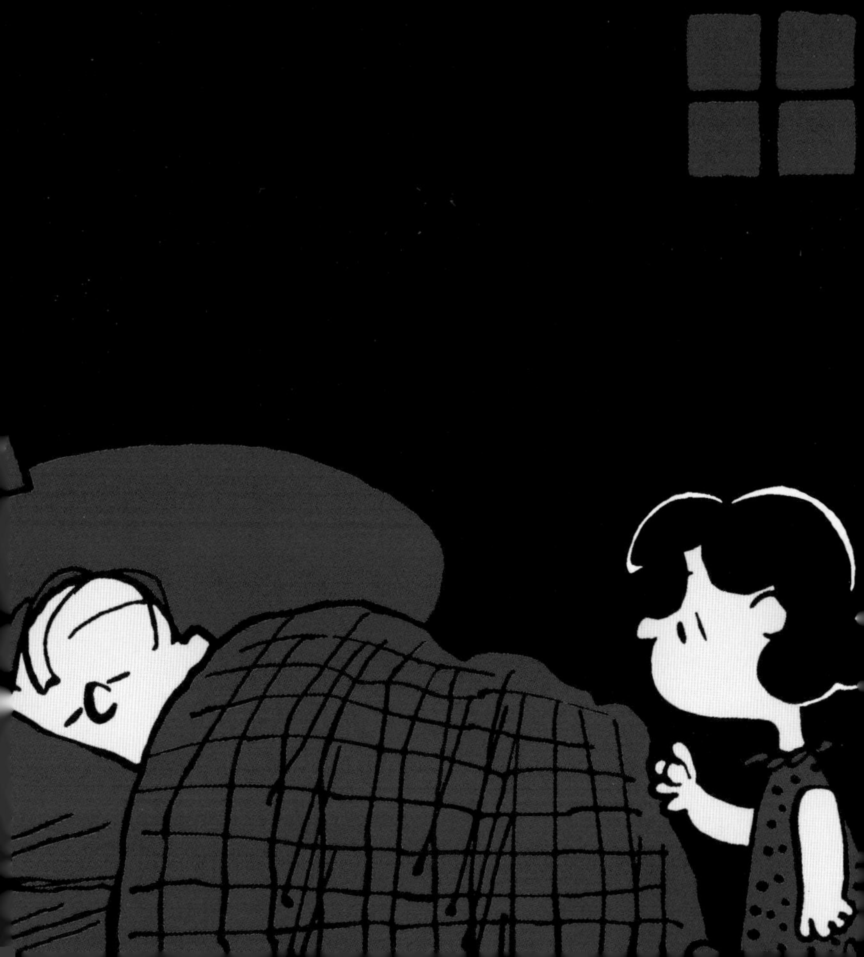

love is

committing yourself in writing

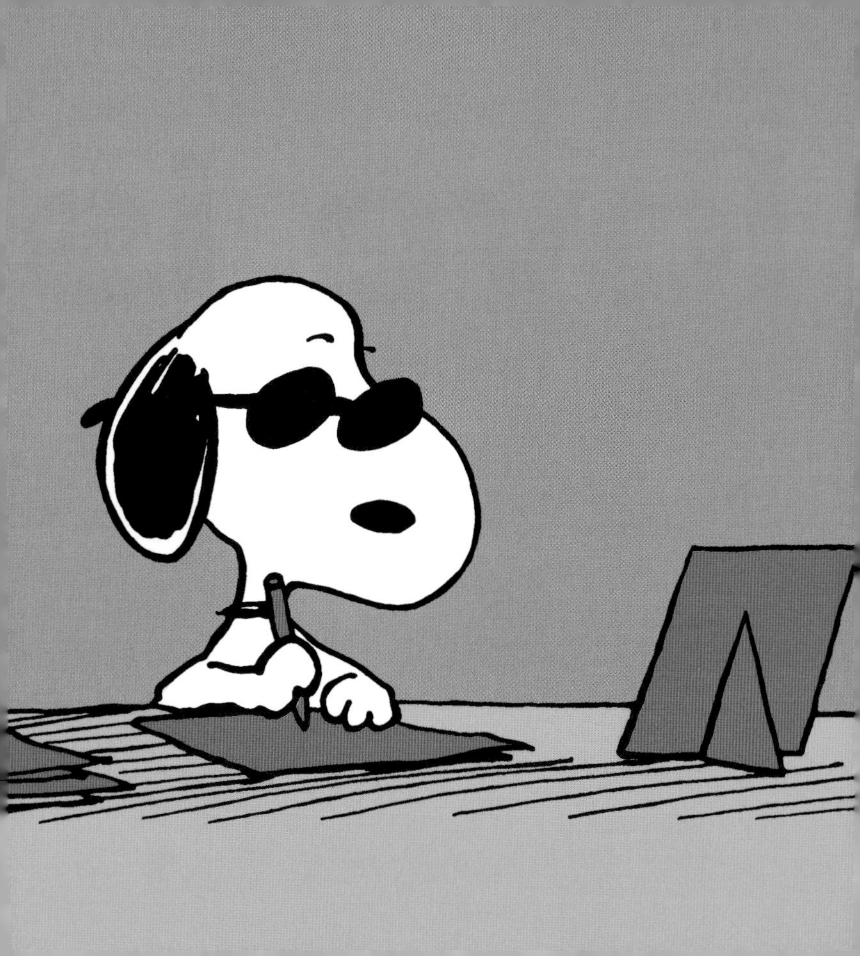

love is

hating to
say goodbye

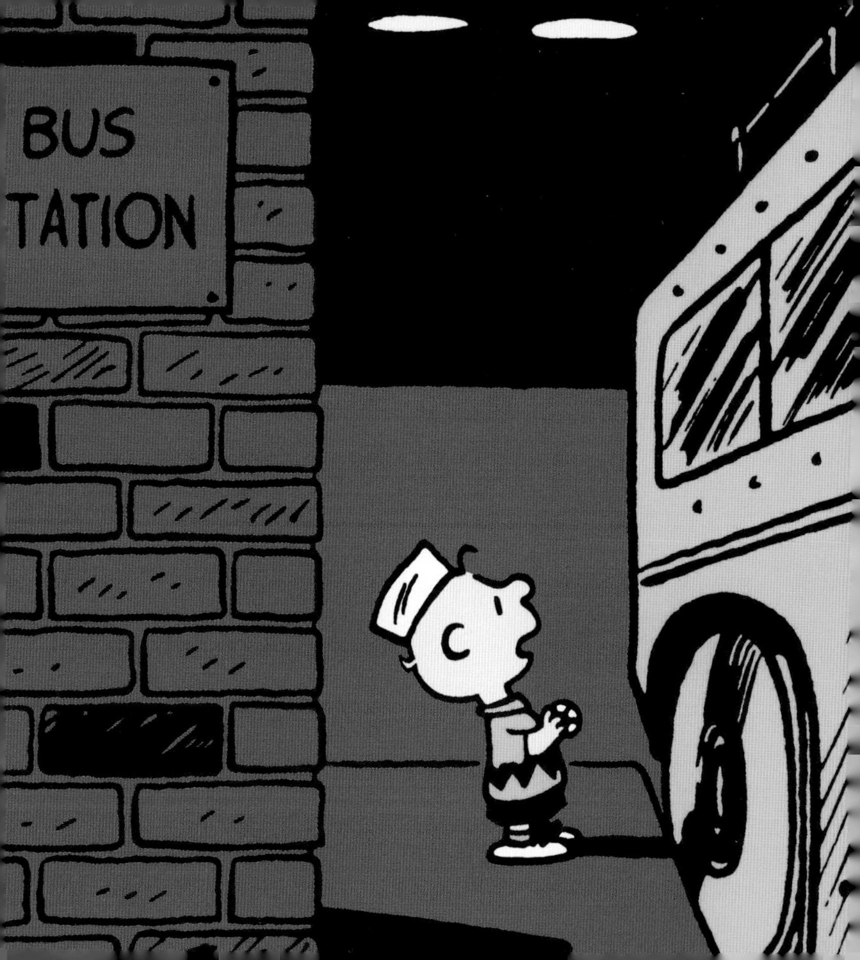
BUS
TATION

love is

messing up
someone's
hair

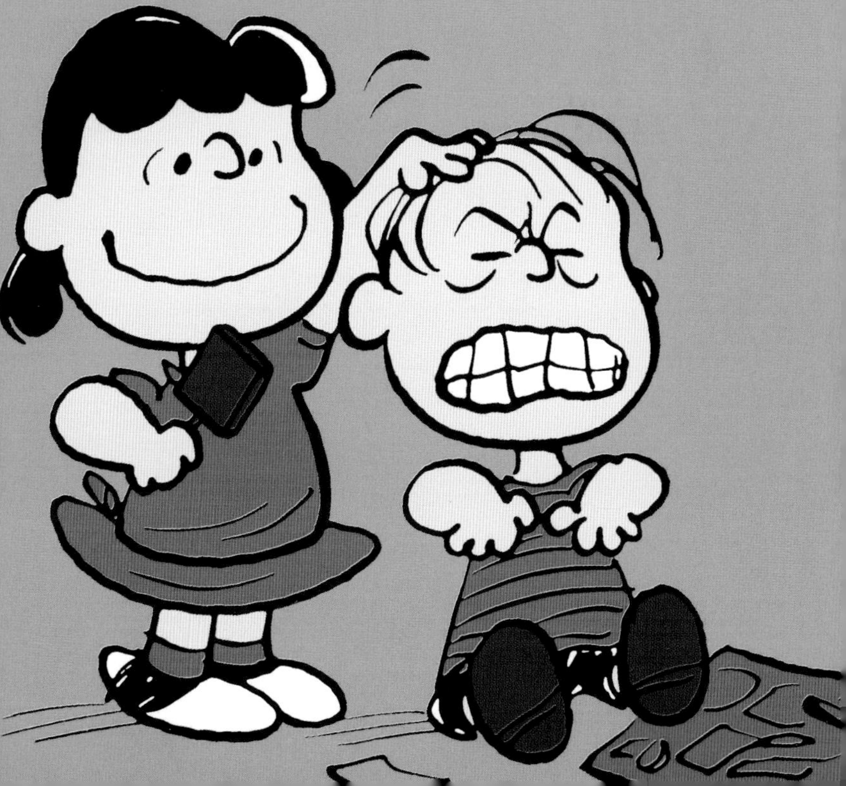

love is

lending your
best comic
magazines

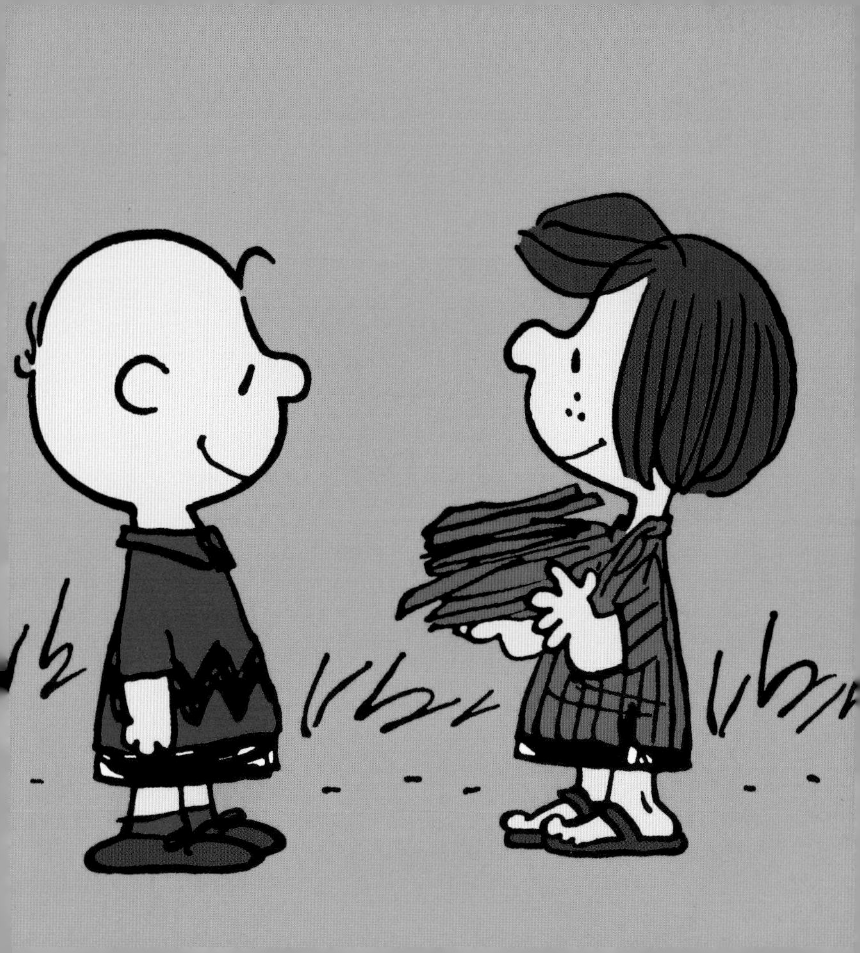

love is

walking
hand-in-hand

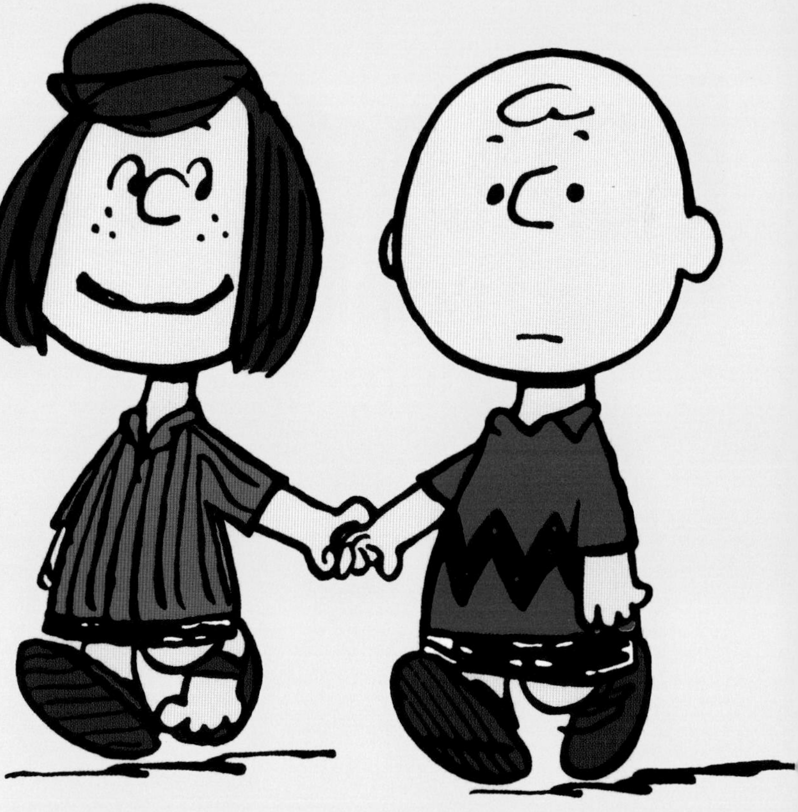

love is

helping your
sister with her
homework

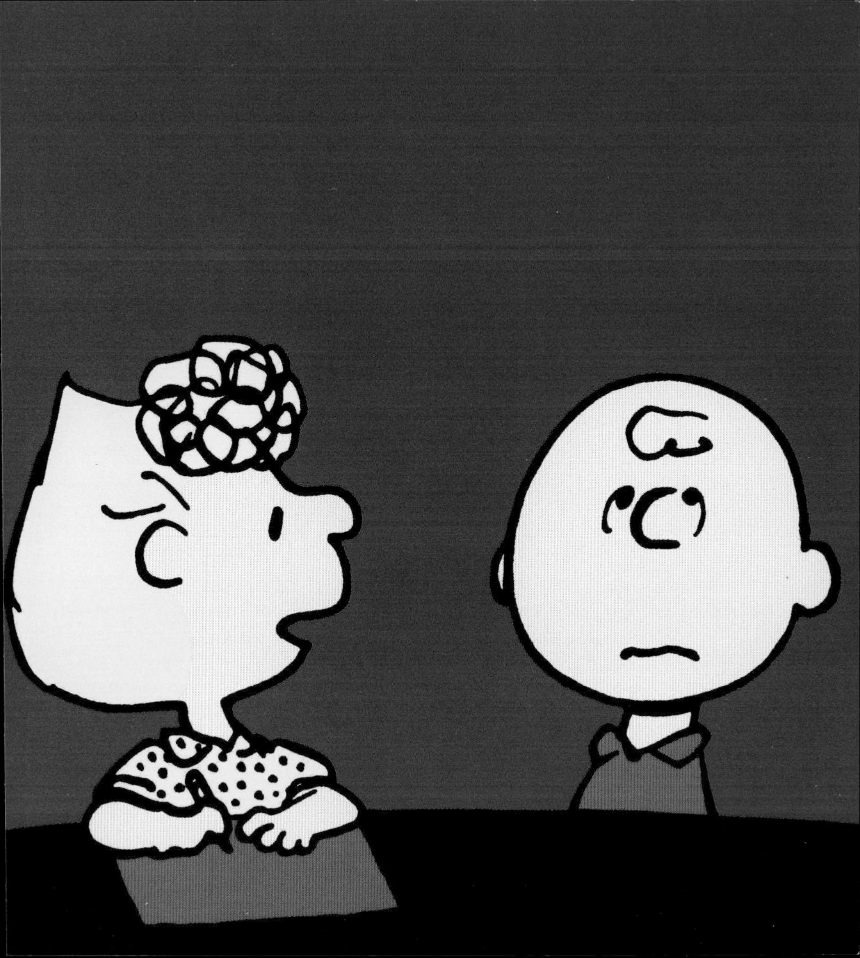

love is

a letter on
pink stationery

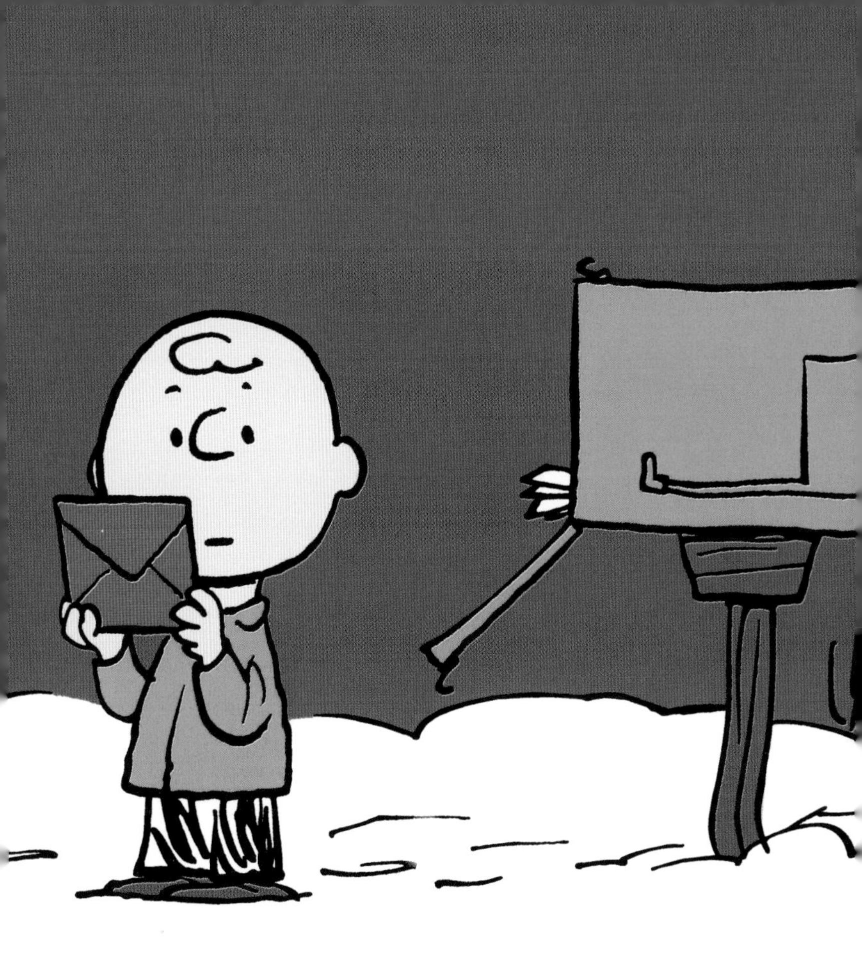

love is

being a good
watch dog

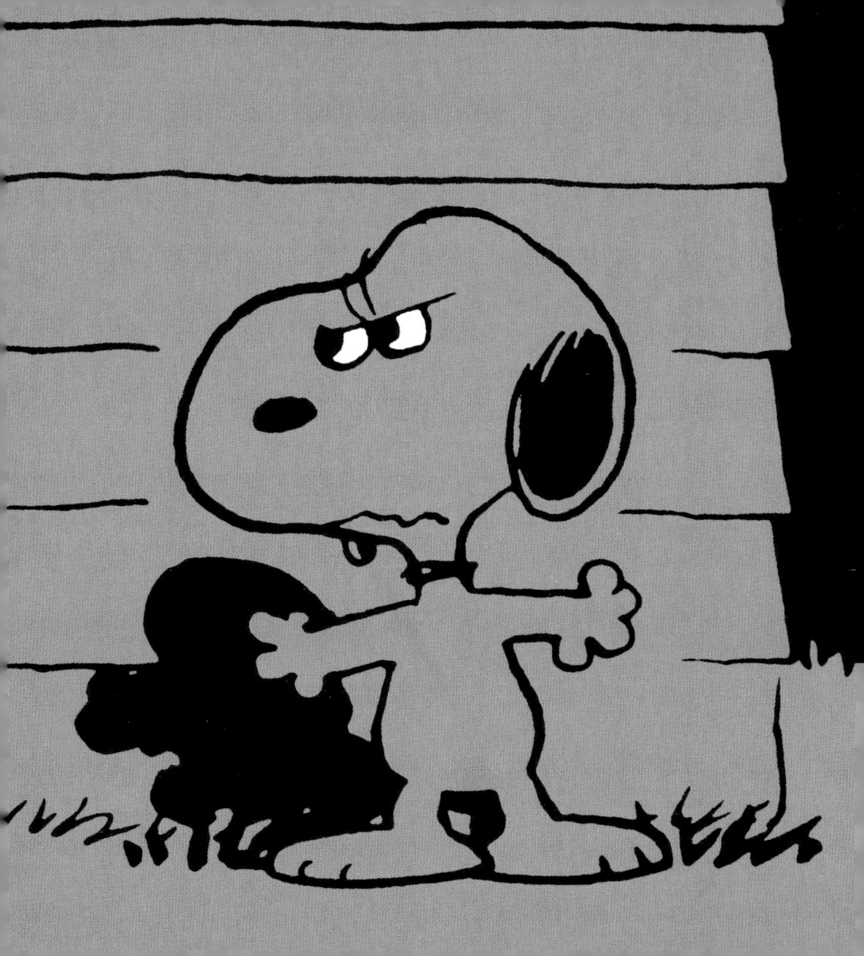

love is

wishing you had
nerve enough to
go over and talk
with that little
girl with the
red hair

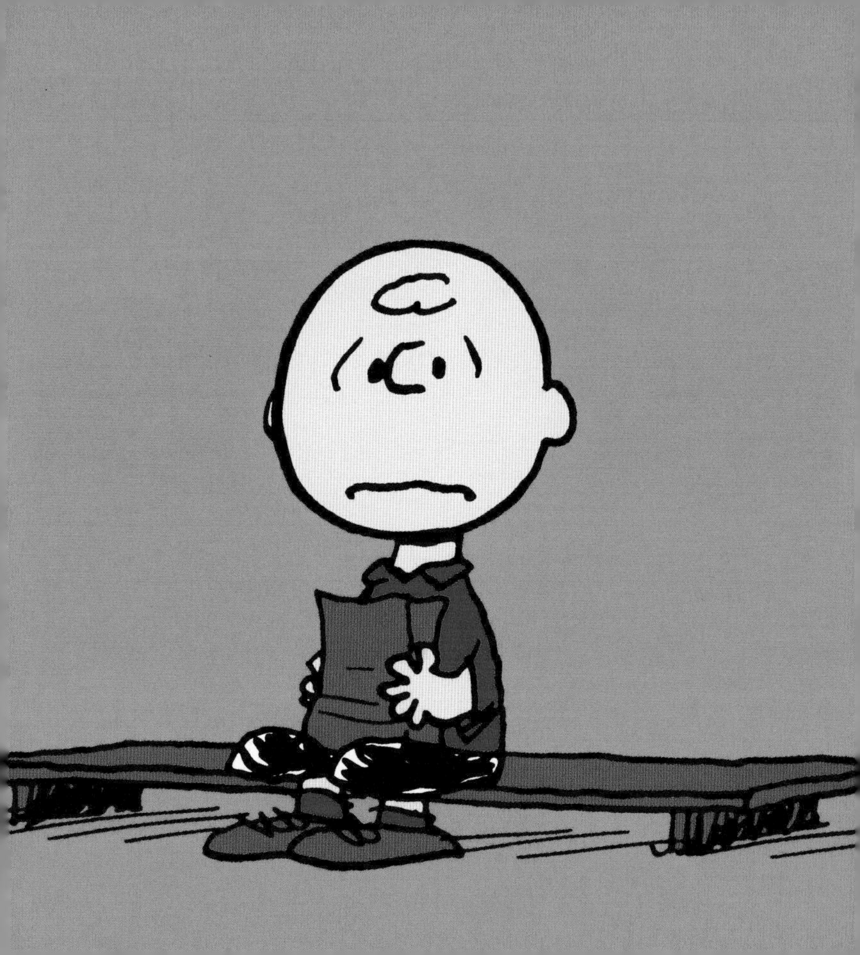

love is

being patient
with your
little brother

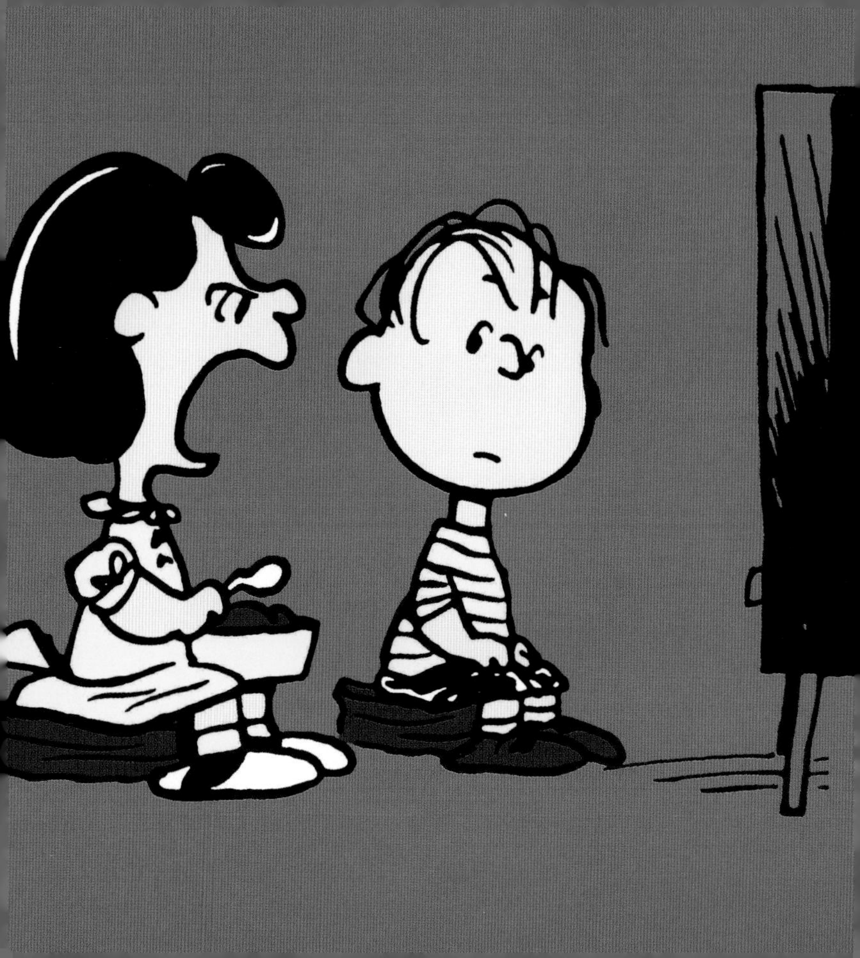

love is

dancing
cheek-to-cheek

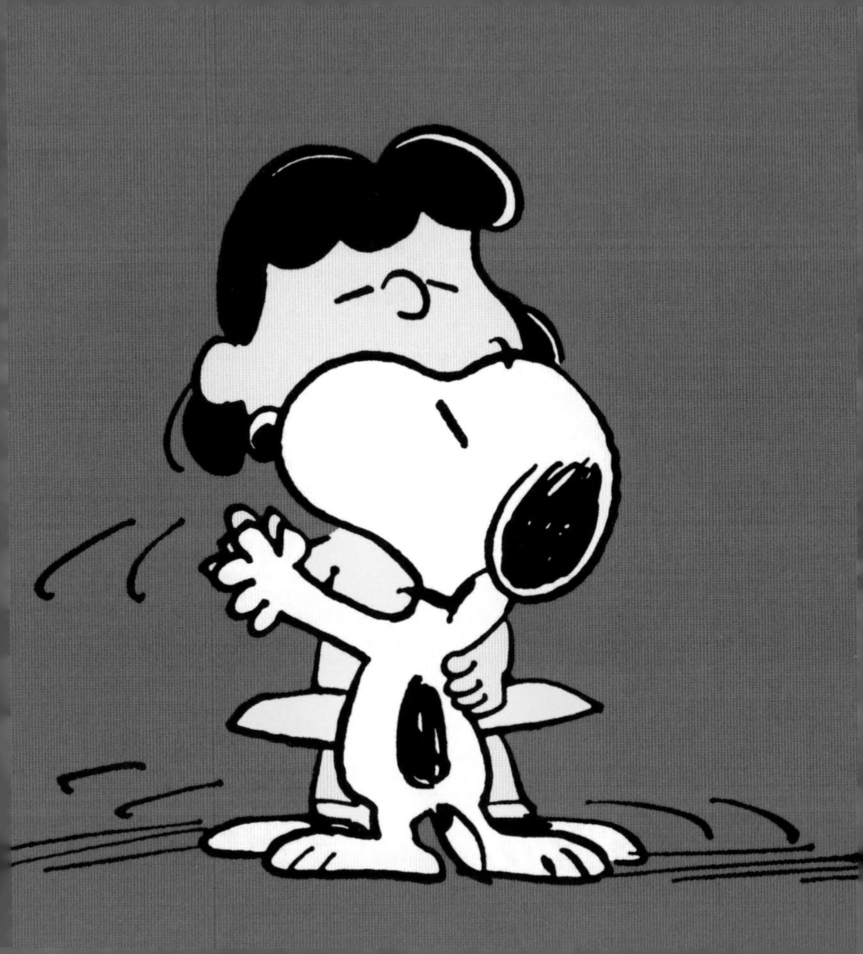

love is

standing in a doorway just to see if she comes walking by

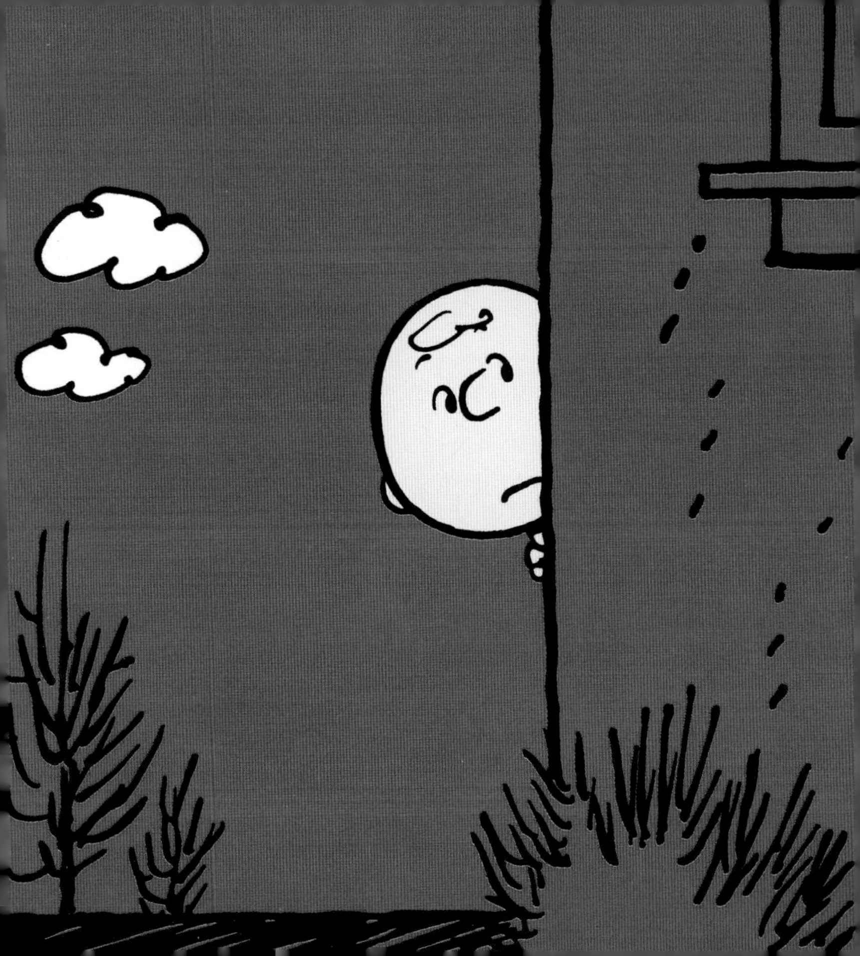

love is

a goodnight
kiss

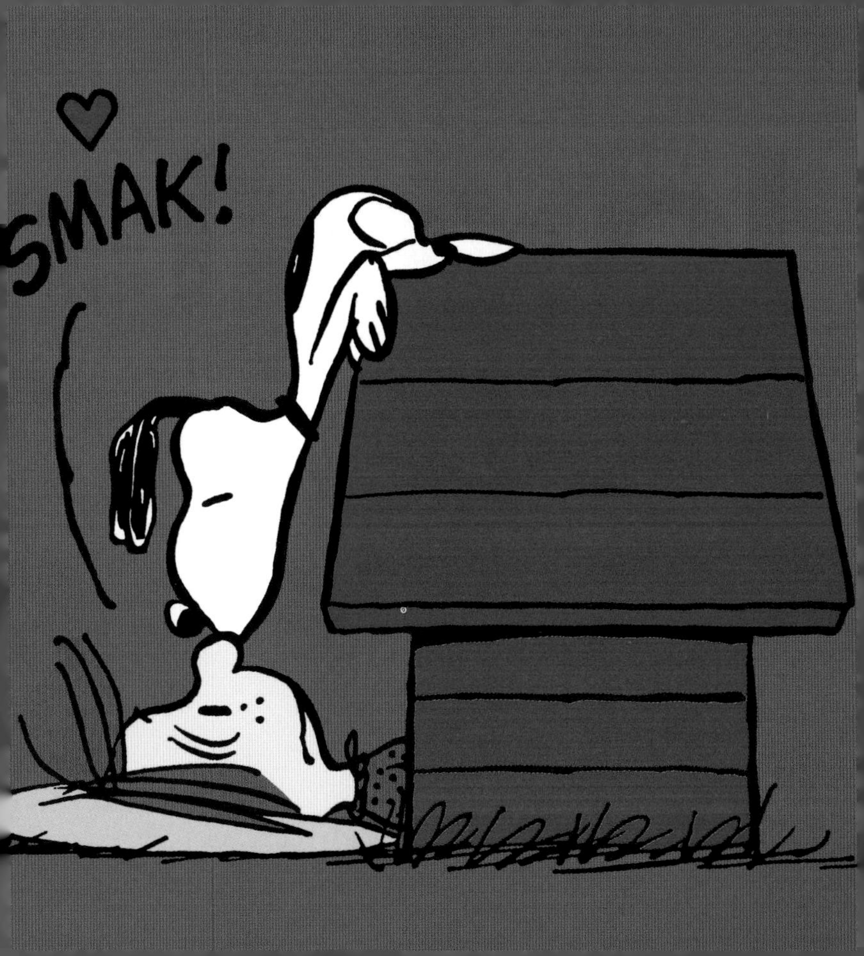
SMAK!

love is

a smile
even when he
keeps you
waiting

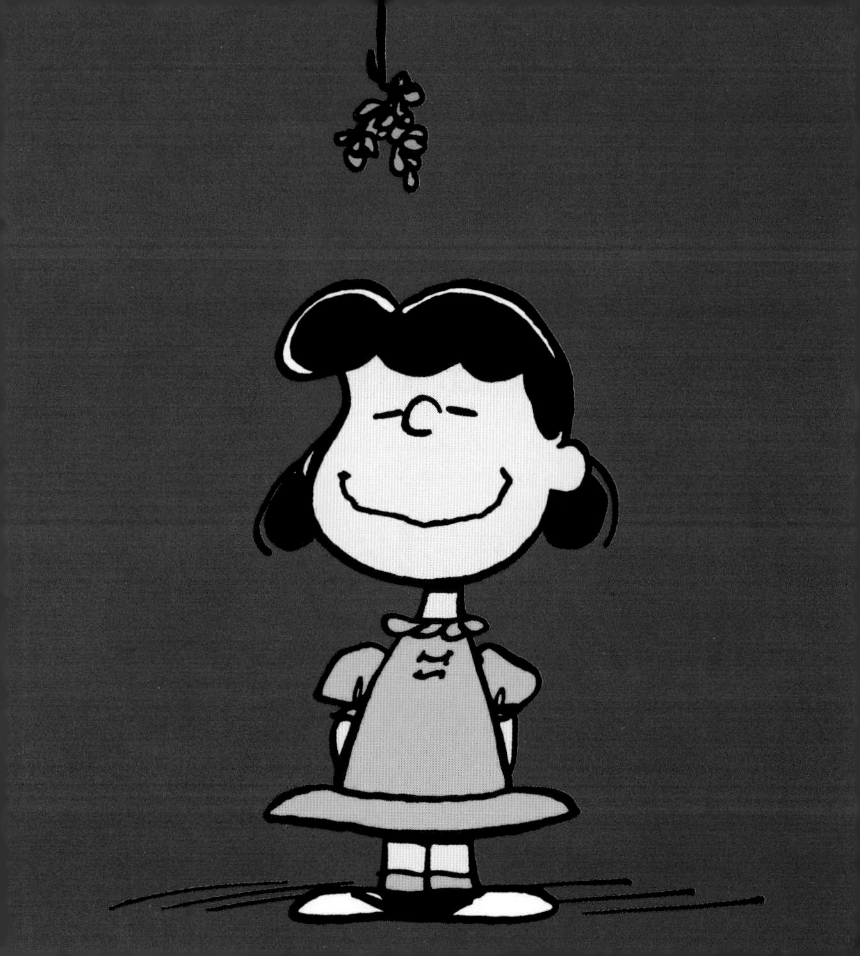

love is
the whole world

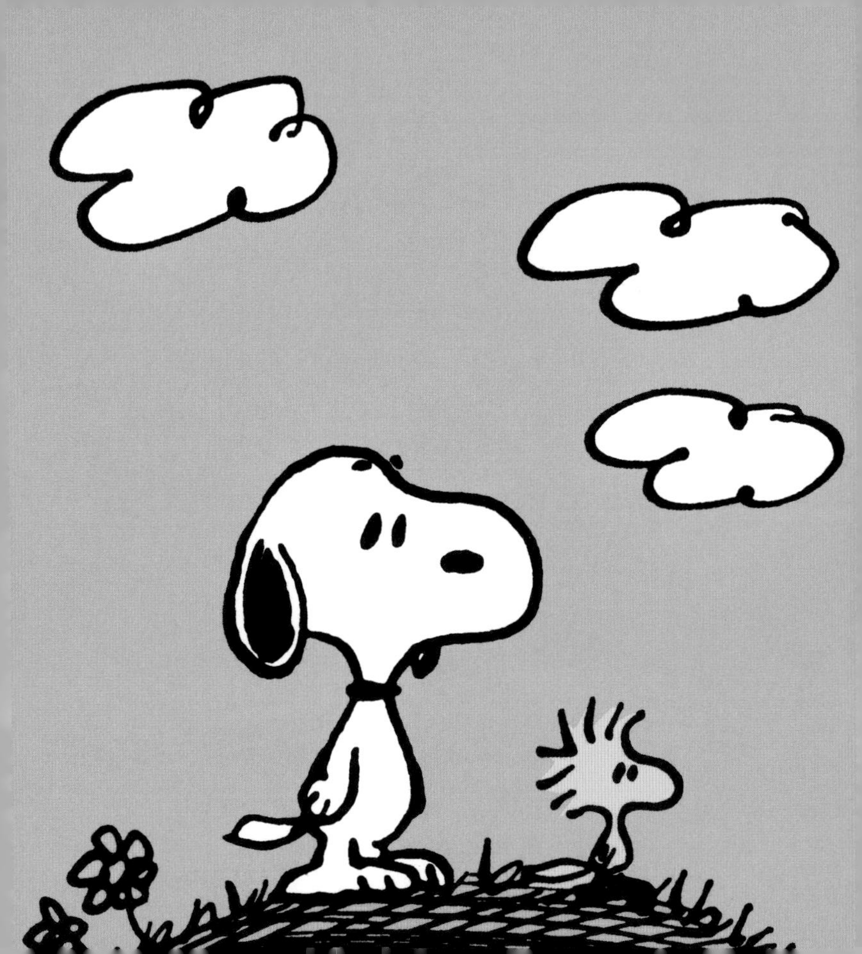

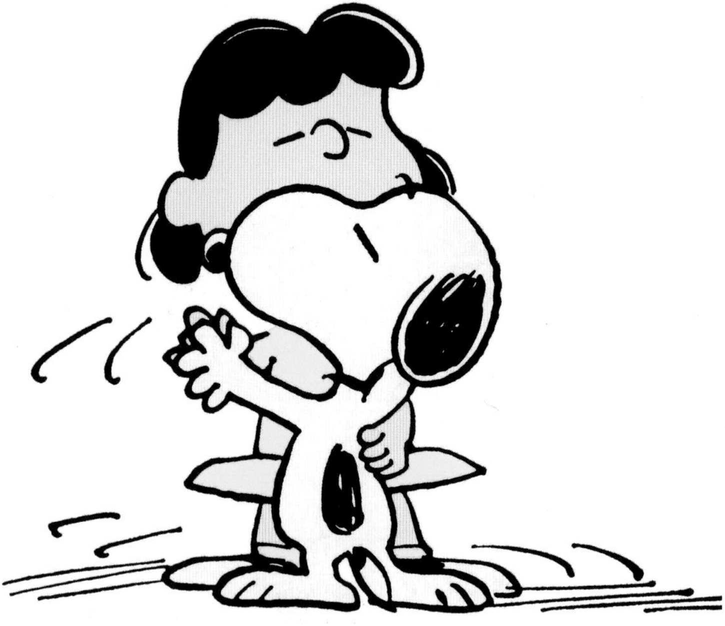

Ravette Publishing Ltd
Unit 3, Tristar Centre, Star Road
Partridge Green, West Sussex RH13 8RA
Tel: 01403 711443   Email: ravettepub@aol.com